MEAN MACHINES

MILITARY AIRCRAFT

PAUL DOWSWELL

Raintree

Chicago, Illinois

© 2005 Raintree
Published by Raintree,
A division of Reed Elsevier, Inc.
Chicago, IL

For information, address the publisher:
Raintree, 100 N. LaSalle, Suite 1200
Chicago, IL 60602
Customer Service: 888-363-4266
Visit our website at www.raintreelibrary.com

Printed and bound in China by South China Printing Company
09 08 07 06 05
10 9 8 7 6 5 4 3 2 1

Library of Congress Cataloging-in-Publication Data
Dowswell, Paul.
 Military aircraft / Paul Dowswell.
  p. cm. -- (Mean machines)
 ISBN 1-4109-1081-4 (library binding - hardcover) -- ISBN 1-4109-1196-9
(pbk.) 1. Airplanes, Military--Juvenile literature. I. Title. II.
Series.
 UG1240.D68 2004
 623.74'6--dc22

                    2004015339

Acknowledgments
The publishers would like to thank the following for permission to reproduce photographs:
akg-images: pp. **20** (b), **20–21**, **54** (b); AVPIX: p. **4** (Austin J. Brown); AVPIX/John Stroud Collection: pp. **32**, **38–39**; Bettmann/Corbis: pp. **11**, **11** (b), **12** (t), **13**, **14** (b), **23**, **26** (b), **32–33**, **42**, **46**; Corbis: pp. **12–13**, **22**, **26–27**, **33** (r), **38**; Corbis/George Hall: pp. **5** (t,r), **40–41**, **46–47**, **50–51**; Corbis Saba: p. **53** (m) (Thomas Hartwell); Corbis Sygma: p. **57** (Alain Nogues); Getty Images: pp. **21**, **22–23**; Hulton-Deutsch Collection/Corbis: pp. **8**, **10**, **36–37**, **52** (l); Imperial War Museum: p. **37** (r), **50** (l); Military Picture Library: pp. **5**, **8–9**, **14–15**, **16** (b), **16–17**, **17** (t), **28–29**, **30–31**, **31** (t), **34**, **39**, **45**, **54–55**, **55** (b), **56** (b); Military Picture Library/Corbis: pp. **6–7** (Robin Adshead), **28** (t) (Graham Wheatley), **53** (b) (Robin Adshead); Museum of Flight/Corbis: pp. **15** (t), **24** (t), **24–25**, **25** (r), **36** (t), **44**; Novosti: pp. **5** (b,r), **43**, **44–45**, **56–57**; Reuters/Corbis: p. **47** (t); Science & Society Picture Library: p. **18**; US Air Force: pp. **30** (l), **41** (Jerry Morrison); USAF Photo: p. **27** (r) (contributed by Billy Rawl, Pilot, 100th Air Refuelling Squadron 1961–65); U.S. Navy: **title page** (David Rush), pp. **5** (m,r), **9** (Chris Howell), **18–19** (Stephanie M. Bergman), **34–35** (Scott A. Moak), **35** (David Rush), **40** (t) (Ensign John Gay), **42–43** (Paul Farley), **61** (Paul Farley), **48** (l), **48–49** (Damon J. Moritz), **49**, **51** (DoD), **52** (b).

Cover photograph of a Lockheed Martin F-177A reproduced with permission of Aviation Images (Mark Wagner)

Every effort has been made to contact copyright holders of any material reproduced in this book. Any omissions will be rectified in subsequent printings if notice is given to the publishers.

The paper used to print this book comes from sustainable resources.

CONTENTS

Any words appearing in the text in bold, **like this,** are explained in the glossary. You can also look out for them in the "Up to Speed" box at the bottom of each page.

WHAT ARE WARPLANES?

The air show crowd is getting restless. An *F-15 Eagle* fighter is due to make an appearance, but it is nowhere to be seen. Then, a distant whine is heard. Eyes scan the sky. Within a second, a jet comes crashing though the air to swoop low over the crowd with a loud roar.

The ground shakes as one of the most expensive machines on Earth thunders overhead. The plane loops, twists, and turns. Then, it stands on its tail and shoots to the top of the sky. In less than a minute, it is gone. All that's left is the strong smell of burned fuel. Seeing such an amazing sight, it is hard to believe that the first planes flew only a century ago.

THE FRENCH NIEUPORT 17

This was one of the first fighters of World War I. It could fly at 120 **mph** (190 km/h). It had a **machine gun** mounted on the top wing above the **cockpit.** The pilot could fire the gun while sitting, but he had to stand up to reload with **ammunition.**

UP TO SPEED   machine gun   gun that can fire bullets very quickly in a row

FIGHTERS AND BOMBERS

During World War I (1914–1918), two main types of warplanes were invented. One type was the fighter. This was designed to destroy other enemy aircraft and gain control of the sky. The other type was the bomber. This was made to drop explosives on the enemy's troops, cities, and factories.

Warplanes were also used for **reconnaissance,** ground support (helping troops fighting on the ground), and carrying supplies. Today, it is impossible to imagine fighting a war without aircraft. But types of aircraft have changed a lot since World War I.

FIND OUT LATER . . .

Which plane can fly over three times the speed of sound?

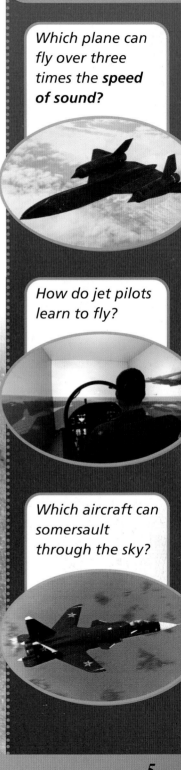

How do jet pilots learn to fly?

Which aircraft can somersault through the sky?

A U.S. Air Force *F-15E Eagle* in action, during the Gulf War of 1991.

reconnaissance   keeping watch on an enemy's movements and strength

AERIAL BASICS

From the first clumsy **biplanes** to the latest jets, warplanes throughout the 20th century have had a lot in common. Fighters have to be fast and highly **maneuverable.** This gives a pilot the best possible chance to survive in a fight with an enemy. Bombers have to travel long distances and carry heavy loads. The labels marked on the British Royal Air Force *Tornado* below show the names of important aircraft parts.

PROPELLER ENGINE

The first aircraft used engines similar to those in cars. These are called **internal combustion** engines. They work by exploding a small amount of fuel, which moves a **piston.** This turns a **crankshaft,** which then spins a **propeller.** The spinning propeller pulls the aircraft through the air.

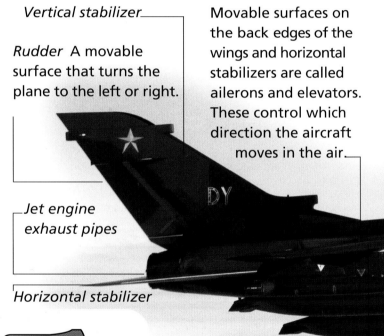

Vertical stabilizer

Rudder A movable surface that turns the plane to the left or right.

Movable surfaces on the back edges of the wings and horizontal stabilizers are called ailerons and elevators. These control which direction the aircraft moves in the air.

Jet engine exhaust pipes

Horizontal stabilizer

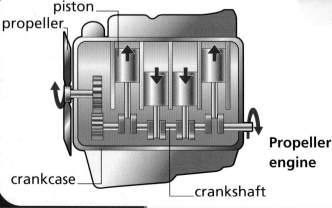

piston

propeller

crankcase

crankshaft

Propeller engine

Wing Fighter jets have **swept-back wings.** This helps them fly faster.

biplane   plane with two sets of wings, one above the other
maneuverable   able to turn or change direction easily

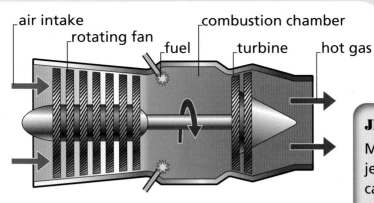

air intake
rotating fan
fuel
combustion chamber
turbine
hot gas

Turbojet engine

Ejector seat All jet fighter planes have special seats that can throw the **crew** away from the aircraft in an emergency.

The tip of a plane is called its nose. Some fighter jets have a powerful gun, or **cannon,** in the nose.

Fuselage The main body of the aircraft.

Cockpit The crew sits in here.

Weapons load Most modern jets carry missiles and bombs underneath their wings and fuselage.

Insignia These markings show friend and enemy which country the plane represents.

Air intake Air is sucked in here and into the jet engine.

JET ENGINE

Modern military jets have engines called turbojets. Air is sucked into them through a fan and then squeezed into a combustion chamber. Fuel mixes in with the air and **ignites.** Hot gases rush out of the back and drive the jet forward.

swept-back wings wings that make a V or triangular shape against the body of an airplane

LEARNING TO FLY

The act of flying military aircraft has always been risky. In World War I, half of all the 22,000 British pilots who flew in the war were killed. Many of them died in flying accidents. Flying warplanes can still be a highly dangerous job— with or without a war to fight. Ever since planes first took to the sky, learning how to fly them has been a matter of a teacher and student going up together. Special training aircraft are used with two sets of controls, one for the teacher and one for the student. The first solo flight is one of the most stressful experiences in a pilot's life.

FLIGHT PIONEERS

These American World War I pilots are learning to fly combat aircraft. Despite the terrible dangers, they were not given parachutes. The idea was to make them try to land even a badly damaged aircraft safely, rather than jump out and destroy the plane.

Pilots learn to fly the *Harrier* VTOL jet with this two-seater version.

propeller   spinning blade that pulls an aircraft through the air

JET BOYS AND GIRLS

Learning to fly military jets is a long and difficult process. Trainee pilots have to be physically tough to put up with the stress of being thrown around the sky in a plane. They also need to have perfect eyesight and color vision. Trainees start off on slow-moving **propeller** aircraft before moving to trainer jets. Finally, they move up to two-seater versions of the powerful military aircraft they are going to fly. Even when a trainee is an official pilot, he or she still spends a lot of flying time doing training exercises. These develop the skills and lessons needed to fly safely.

HIGH-TECH VIDEO GAME

Today, pilots do part of their training on hi-tech computer-controlled flight **simulators**. A video screen shows a realistic image of what it is like looking out of a **cockpit** window. The flight simulator moves around like a real plane when the trainee moves the controls.

simulator   device that copies the conditions of an actual situation

FLYING HERO

Douglas Bader, below, was a British fighter pilot who lost both his legs in a flying accident in 1931. He was not going to let that stop him from flying. He became a squadron leader in the Battle of Britain in 1940. He was shot down in 1941 and captured by the Germans. He tried to escape several times, but did not succeed.

ACES AND HEROES

World War I was like a nightmare for the soldiers of both sides. They lived and fought in muddy **trenches.** Millions of men were killed by **machine guns, artillery** shells, and poisonous gases. Fighter pilots were different. They fought one to one in the clear blue sky. It was in this war that the idea of the "ace" first came up. French pilots had to shoot down five enemy planes to be called an ace. German and British pilots had to shoot down ten.

>>>>>>>>>>>>>
Find out more about the Battle of Britain on page 15.

speed of sound   how fast sound travels
squadron   fighting group or unit in an air force

THE RED BARON

The most famous ace of World War I was a German named Manfred von Richthofen. He was known as the Red Baron, after the color of the red Fokker *Dreidecker* **triplane** he flew. During the war, the Red Baron shot down 80 planes belonging to the **Allies.** He flew with a **squadron** that was known as Richthofen's Flying Circus because its planes were brightly colored. He was shot down and killed behind British lines at the end of the war.

World War II (1939–1945) had its share of aces, too. The most successful was the German pilot Erich Hartmann. He shot down 352 Soviet planes.

The famous German ace Manfred von Richthofen.

GLAMOROUS GLENNIS

Chuck Yeager was an American **test pilot.** In 1947 he became the first person to fly an aircraft faster than the **speed of sound.** He made the flight in the **rocket-propelled** *X-1.* This was named *Glamorous Glennis,* after his wife. At the time, flying at such speeds was very dangerous. Planes would fall apart in flight or go into uncontrollable spins that ended in fiery explosions.

triplane   plane with three sets of wings on each side

FIGHTERS

Military leaders quickly got the idea that planes could help them fight wars. They were first used in World War I as **reconnaissance** aircraft. Soldiers heading for positions on the **front lines** soon came to fear the sound of an enemy aircraft above their heads. After the aircraft had gone, they could expect attack. Reconnaissance planes were such a problem that a new kind of aircraft was invented to drive them from the sky: the fighter.

FOUR WINGS

Most warplanes of World War I were **biplanes.** This means they had two sets of wings. This Sopwith *Camel* was a successful British design. Aircraft like this were used to defend London from German *Gotha* bombers.

UP TO SPEED   front line   place on a battlefield where the two sides meet

WORLD WAR I FIGHTERS

In World War I, pilots first fought each other with pistols, rifles, or even grappling hooks (hooks that look like an anchor on the end of a rope or chain). Not surprisingly, these weapons did not cause a lot of damage.

Machine guns, firing hundreds of bullets a minute, were more deadly weapons. These were fitted on the top wing, or in a second **cockpit** behind the pilot. Just in front of the pilot would have been the best place to put a gun. He could then point his plane at the enemy and fire. But, at the start of the war, this would have meant that the pilot could have possibly shot off his own **propeller.**

Fokker **triplanes** were some of the most **maneuverable** warplanes of their time.

FIRING THROUGH THE PROPELLER

The then-German (now Dutch) Fokker aircraft company solved the problem of firing through the propeller in 1915. They invented a device that timed the firing of bullets so they passed between the propeller blades. The picture above shows an early American version of this type of machine gun.

WORLD WAR II FIGHTERS

Fighter planes changed a lot in the twenty years between the two world wars. Open **cockpits** were covered with a **Plexiglas** screen. This meant pilots had a less chilly and windy flight. Instead of two sets of wings, most planes had one set of wings. The fighter's guns were usually inside the wings. The pilot fired the guns using a control in the cockpit. These fighters were also considerably faster and deadlier than the planes of World War I.

LITTLE FRIENDS

The *P-51 Mustang*, made by a company called North American, was one of the best American fighter planes of World War II. This plane was used to protect slow-moving bombers from German and Japanese fighters. It carried extra fuel in tear-shaped tanks under the wings. This allowed it to fly for up to eight hours. By the end of the war, *Mustangs* could fly with American bombers from England to Berlin, Germany.

This picture shows a *Spitfire* (front) during the Battle of Britain.

cockpit   area where the crew sits and controls the airplane

BATTLE OF BRITAIN

The first full-scale air battle in history was fought in the summer of 1940. It was called the Battle of Britain. Germany tried to destroy the British Royal Air Force. If it had succeeded, Germany would have gone on to invade and conquer Great Britain. But the British Royal Air Force had two excellent fighter planes called the *Hurricane* and the *Spitfire*. The *Hurricane* was steady, rugged, and effective. The *Spitfire* was so fast and **maneuverable** it could fly rings around its opponents. Many people think it is one of the most beautiful aircraft ever built.

FAST BUT FATAL

The Japanese Mitsubishi *A6M Zero* was one of the fastest and most maneuverable fighters of the part of World War II fought in the Pacific. But there was a catch. To save weight to help it fly faster, it had no armor to protect the pilot. It carried no radio and had a fuel tank that often burst into flames. Japanese fighter pilots discovered that their *Zero* could be shot down very easily.

Plexiglas   transparent, tough, plasticlike resin used instead of glass to make windows or cockpit covers in aircraft

MODERN JET FIGHTERS

The first military jets were flown by the Germans near the end of World War II. Germany attacked U.S. bomber formations with the *Me 262*. This two-engine jet was almost impossible to shoot down because it moved so much faster than any other plane in the sky. Surprisingly, pilots of the *Me 262* found it difficult to shoot down the slow-moving bombers. They did not have enough time to line up their planes to get an accurate shot as they zoomed past. The first battles between jets took place during the Korean War (1950–1953).

TOP SELLER

The *MiG-21* is the best-selling jet fighter ever made. During the **Cold War,** the Soviets built more than 15,000. They sold the planes to countries all over the world.

Cold War   years between 1946 and 1989 when the Soviet Union and the United States and its allies did not like or trust each other

SPEED OF SOUND

Jet engines became more powerful after World War II. It was soon possible for aircraft to fly faster than the **speed of sound.** It is now common for jet fighters to fly at 1,000 **mph** (1,600 km/h) or faster. Single-seater jet fighters, such as the American *F-16* or Russian *MiG-25,* now weigh as much as a World War II bomber did. They are much more complicated pieces of machinery. These amazing planes can travel 3,280 feet (1,000 meters) in less than two seconds.

The *F-16* is one of the most effective fighters ever.

TOP CLIMBER

This *Electric Lightning* is a type of jet called an **interceptor.** It climbs to great heights in a matter of minutes to intercept enemy bombers or fighters. Its design is unusual. It has two jet engines placed on top of each other. This makes the *Lightning* surprisingly thin.

---

interceptor   type of jet fighter that can climb and fly very quickly to cut off enemy aircraft

VTOL JETS

Aircraft need a runway to land and take off. This can be awkward for military aircraft. A runway near the enemy's **front line** is large and **vulnerable** to air attacks and **artillery.** Helicopters can take off and land from a much smaller area, but they are no match for any **high-performance** enemy jet fighter. This is why the **vertical** takeoff and landing (VTOL) jet is such a useful idea. These aircraft can take off and land straight upward and downward, just like helicopters.

A DREAM TO FLY?

This weird and wonderful machine was an early British experiment in vertical takeoff aircraft. It was nicknamed the Flying Bedstead.

artillery   large, land-based guns
thrust   force produced by a jet aircraft to propel it through the sk

HOVER CRAFT

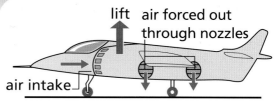

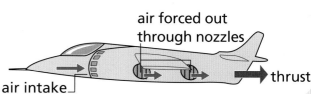

Like a helicopter, a VTOL jet can take off and land in a very tight space. Also, like a helicopter, it can hover in the air. These aircraft first appeared in the 1960s. British and Soviet air forces each had their own versions. The Soviets had the Yakovlev *Yak 36*. The British had the Hawker Siddeley *Harrier* jump jet. The United States military also bought the *Harrier*. The *Harrier* cannot fly as fast as most other modern jet fighters, but it is very **maneuverable** and is a good combat aircraft.

HOW THE ENGINE WORKS

The *Harrier* jet **thrust** comes out of four rotating **nozzles** on the side of the aircraft. When the pilot wants to take off or land, he or she places the nozzles in a downward position. When the pilot wants to fly forward, the nozzles point backward.

A *Harrier* VTOL jet takes off from an American **aircraft carrier**.

vertical straight upward
vulnerable easy to attack or shoot down, not well-protected

19

BOMBERS

The first **strategic bombers** were strange, gas-filled balloons that were the size of cruise ships. They were called zeppelins, after their inventor and manufacturer, Count Ferdinand von Zeppelin. Instead of wings, they used huge bags of **hydrogen** to lift them into the air. They also had **propeller** engines to push them through the sky. They could travel for hundreds of miles without refueling. At first, the Germans built them as **reconnaissance** craft for the navy. Then, they decided to use them to drop bombs on enemy cities.

IN CONTROL

The control cabin of a Zeppelin (see below) was cold and very noisy. When the Zeppelin's engines were running, the crew could barely hear themselves speak. There were no seats or parachutes. This saved weight for important cargo such as bombs.

A Zeppelin on the way to attack England.

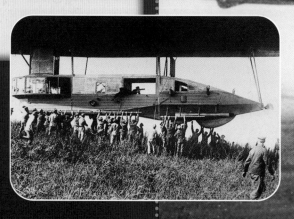

UP TO SPEED incendiary bullet bullet that bursts into flames when fired from a gun

ATTACK AND DEFENSE

The first zeppelin raids took place on Paris and London in 1915. They caused a lot of fear and panic among the helpless people below, but they did much less damage than intended. This was because zeppelins could carry only a small number of bombs. At first, these huge machines were impossible to shoot down. They flew too high for fighters to reach. But by late 1916, British fighters such as the *BE-2* **biplane** could catch up with them. Pilots fighting zeppelins fired **incendiary bullets** from **machine guns.** These bullets glowed white hot when shot from the gun. They set fire to the hydrogen gas inside the zeppelin. This caused a huge explosion that destroyed the zeppelins.

THE CLOUD CAR

This tiny carriage contained a member of the crew. It dangled from a Zeppelin hidden in a cloud, out of sight of enemy aircraft or **antiaircraft guns.** The man inside the cloud car used a telephone line to the zeppelin's pilot to guide the craft along.

strategic bomber bomber that attacks an enemy's home, rather than being used on the battlefield

WORLD WAR I BOMBERS

Zeppelins terrified the people of enemy cities. But they were slow and very expensive. They became easy to shoot down and could only carry a small number of bombs. So the countries fighting World War I began to invent aircraft that could travel faster, carry more bombs, and be more difficult to shoot down. The first winged bombers were big but clumsy-looking machines, such as the German Zeppelin-Staaken *R* and the British Handley Page *0/100*. These aircraft could carry a deadly load of up to 2 tons (1.8 metric tons) of bombs. They also had room for three or more machine gunners to defend the bomber against attacking fighters.

DON'T HIT THE WING!

The first bombers were ordinary **reconnaissance** or fighter planes. The pilot or air gunner dropped a couple of handheld bombs out of his open cockpit. These missiles were hardly more destructive than a hand grenade.

Gotha bombers like this attacked Paris and London.

UP TO SPEED antiaircraft guns   guns made to defend against an air attack

DROPPING BOMBS

During World War I, the bomber's pilot or air gunner dropped the first bombs from the aircraft's open **cockpit**. Later, bombs were fitted under the wings.

By 1918 specially built bombers had their own bomb bays. These were sections of the planes designed to carry bombs. Aircraft such as these had a **crew** of four or more men. Not all World War I bombers were like these sturdy planes. Some, such as the British Sopwith *1½ Strutter* or French Breguet *14*, were almost the same size as fighters. They had only one or two pilots and carried fewer bombs. Aircraft such as these were much more **maneuverable**, so they were harder to shoot down.

CREATURES OF THE NIGHT

The big World War I bombers, such as this Handley Page *0/400,* were slow and clumsy. This made them easy targets for enemy fighters or **antiaircraft guns.** Because of this, bombers usually operated at night, when it was far more difficult to spot them.

crew   people who operate the aircraft

WORLD WAR II BOMBERS

Bombers had almost no effect on the countries that fought World War I. But in World War II, they destroyed entire cities.

World War II bombers still had **propeller** engines, but otherwise they changed almost completely. Their **crews** flew inside the planes, rather than in seats open to the air. Instead of a **machine gun** mounted on a rack in an open **cockpit,** two or four machines guns were inside **Plexiglas turrets.** They carried a lot more bombs. The British Handley Page *0/400* bomber of World War I carried about 2,000 pounds (907 kilograms) of bombs. The Avro *Lancaster*, its World War II equivalent, carried at least 7 tons (6.4 metric tons).

TOO SLOW FOR COMFORT

The German Heinkel *He 111* was used successfully at the start of the war in Poland and Western Europe. But during the Battle of Britain in 1940, the *He 111* and other German bombers were too slow and clumsy for faster British fighters, such as the Supermarine *Spitfire* and the Hawker *Hurricane.*

civilian   person not in the military

LONG-RANGE BOMBERS

The most effective bombers of the war were large four-engine aircraft such as the American Boeing *B-17 Flying Fortress* and Consolidated *B-24 Liberator* and the British Handley Page *Halifax* and Avro *Lancaster*. They made medium to long-range journeys. Sometimes hundreds of these aircraft took off from Great Britain's east coast to fly over Germany. Raids like these destroyed German cities such as Dresden and Hamburg and killed hundreds of thousands of **civilians.**

At the end of the war, the U.S. Air Force began using long-range bombers called Boeing *B-29 Superfortresses*. The *B-29* could fly halfway across the Pacific Ocean (three times as far as a *B-17*). It dropped **incendiary bombs** to destroy Japan's cities, which had buildings that were made mainly of wood.

DAY AND NIGHT

In Germany, the U.S. Air Force bombed during the day. British bombers, such as this *Lancaster,* carried out nighttime raids. As a result, Germany had around-the-clock bombing raids against its cities, factories, and fuel supplies.

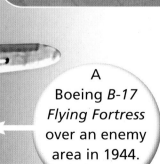

A Boeing *B-17 Flying Fortress* over an enemy area in 1944.

incendiary bomb   bomb that bursts into flames, rather than exploding

THE FIRST ATOMIC BOMBER

An American *B-29* called the *Enola Gay* dropped the first atomic bomb. Here, the pilot is standing next to the plane before the mission. After the bomb attack, one of the **crew** described the city below as looking like a pot of boiling black oil.

ATOMIC BOMBERS

World War II began in 1939 with **squadrons** of German bombers destroying large areas of the Polish capital of Warsaw. It ended in 1945 with two single bombers dropping a bomb each on the Japanese cities of Hiroshima and Nagasaki. Both cities were completely destroyed. The bombs were **atomic bombs.** It had cost $2 billion for scientists in the United States to make them. In 1949 the Soviet Union (Russia and the states it controlled) tested its own atomic bomb. In the early 1950s both the United States and Soviet Union developed the **hydrogen** bomb. This was a new type of atomic weapon. Such bombs were 750 times more powerful than the ones that destroyed Hiroshima and Nagasaki.

atomic bomb   bomb with violent explosive power that is made by scientists

A Soviet *Tu-95* (top) atomic bomber shadowed by American planes.

AVOIDING ENEMY FIRE

After World War II, the United States and Soviet Union became enemies. They did not fight, but a deep dislike developed between them. This was known as the **Cold War.** Both sides had plans to attack each other with hydrogen bombs. Long-range bombers were invented to fly across the world carrying these weapons. These bombers had to fly high and fast. They needed to avoid enemy **interceptor** fighters as well as **antiaircraft guns** and missiles from the ground. By the 1960s, **intercontinental ballistic missiles (ICBMs)** were invented to carry hydrogen bombs long distances without pilots. They could be fired from underground **silos** or **submarines.** Atomic bombers became less important.

intercontinental ballistic missile (ICBM) missile that flies very high up so that it can cross continents

The *Tu-22M/Tu-26 Backfire* is the Russian swing-wing equivalent to the American *F-111*. This aircraft can carry 13 tons (11.8 metric tons) of bombs 7,500 miles (12,000 kilometers).

SWING-WING JETS

Many jet fighters and bombers have **swept-back wings.** This makes a V or triangular shape against the body of the plane. The jets have this design because this wing shape helps the aircraft fly faster. But swept-back wings have one big problem. They do not offer as much **lift** as wings that stick out more. This is especially difficult when the aircraft is taking off or landing. Such jets need long runways and have to travel a long way at high speed before they can take off.

An *F-111* swing-wing bomber with its wings swept forward.

UH
AF
68 062

TECH TALK

Wings
All plane wings have a special curved shape. Air rushes under the bottom of the wing at a higher pressure than air rushing over the top. This produces lift, which gets a plane off the ground.

lift   force that lifts a plane into the air

WINGS OUT

This takeoff and landing problem was solved in the early 1960s with the invention of **swing-wing** jets. For takeoff and landing, these jets bring their wings forward (and out). This means they can take off and land in shorter distances and at lower, safer speeds than if they had their wings swept back. This is especially useful for planes flying long distances, since a plane always uses a large amount of fuel to get into the air.

WINGS IN

Early swing-wing jets such as the American *F-111* and Soviet *Tupolev Tu-22M/Tu-26* needed to fly high and fast, with wings back (or in), until they had almost reached their target areas. Then, they would sneak down very low and slow, with wings forward, under an enemy's **radar,** to launch missiles or drop bombs.

>>>>>>>>>>>>
Find out more about radar on page 53.

SWING-WINGS IN ACTION

OUT
The jet can take off or land at a safe speed.

IN
The jet flies high and fast, escaping enemy attack and going places very quickly.

out

in

in

out

The tailless
Northrop
Grumman *B-2A
Spirit* stealth
bomber is the
latest stealth
design. It is much
bigger than the
Nighthawks
flying with it.
It is said to be
almost impossible
to shoot down,
but at more than
$2 billion a plane,
it should be
very special!

SMALL BOMBERS

Modern bombers carry many different weapons. These modern weapons can hit their targets accurately. This hopefully means that they keep the damage done to nonmilitary buildings to a minimum and cut down the effect on **civilians.**

There are two main types of modern jet bombers. One is the smaller, medium-range aircraft such as the *Jaguar* or *Tornado*. Aircraft such as these perform different tasks. In addition to working as bombers, they are fast and **agile** enough to be fighters, **reconnaissance** aircraft, and ground-support (giving backup to troops on the ground) aircraft. They are not much bigger than jet fighters. Still, they can carry a weapons load as large as a World War II bomber such as the *B-17 Flying Fortress*.

agile   able to move quickly and gracefully

BIG BOMBERS

The most famous large bomber is the U.S. Boeing *B-52 Stratofortress*, which has a range of more than 8,800 miles (14,080 kilometers). This bomber first flew in 1952, and it is expected to still be in use in 2040!

The most modern bombers have features that make them hard to spot by enemy **radar.** The shape of the *F-117 Nighthawk* **stealth** fighter makes it look much smaller on a radar screen than it really is. Its special paint is also designed to soak up radar waves so that it does not reflect back a strong signal.

THE EUROPEAN TORNADO

This small two-person aircraft can fly in all weather and reach targets 800 miles (1,300 kilometers) away. Small bombers like this can cause much more damage than big bombers such as the *B-52*. The *B-52* can carry 5 tons (4.5 metric tons) of bombs. The *Tornado* can carry 9 tons (8.2 metric tons) of mixed bombs and missiles.

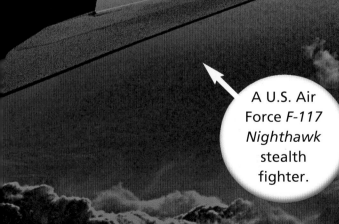

A U.S. Air Force *F-117 Nighthawk* stealth fighter.

stealth   designed to not be seen

ALL AT SEA

GIANT KILLER

Before World War II, the thought of single-engine aircraft destroying a battleship seemed ridiculous. But during the attack on Pearl Harbor, fleets of Nakajima *B5N* "Kate" attack bombers did just that. Most of the ships were sunk by torpedoes from "Kates."

The first takeoff from a ship happened in 1910 on the American cruiser USS *Birmingham*. Warplanes were soon being used for **reconnaissance.** They also attacked enemy ships or other targets.

AIRCRAFT CARRIERS

The first **aircraft carriers** were built during World War I, but too late to play a major part in the war. Between World War I and World War II, the United States, Japan, and Great Britain built up aircraft carrier forces. Japan used its carriers to open World War II in the Pacific. The result was devastating.

This new version of "Kate" was used in the movie *Tora! Tora! Tora!*

aircraft carrier   warship that carries fighter planes to near their target. It is like a movable airfield.

PEARL HARBOR

On December 7, 1941, 183 Japanese planes from six aircraft carriers attacked the United States water and air base in Pearl Harbor, Hawaii. The time was just before 8:00 A.M. An hour later, another force of 167 planes from the same carriers arrived for another attack. The aircraft carried bombs and **torpedoes.** Between them, they sank or seriously damaged eighteen U.S. warships. They also destroyed 174 U.S. aircraft. The attack was one of the most important air battles in history. While the United States was recovering, Japanese soldiers invaded and took over huge areas in the Pacific Ocean.

American battleships after the attack on Pearl Harbor.

UNWILLING HERO

Japanese admiral Yamamoto Isoroku planned the Pearl Harbor attack. It was a great success for Japan. But he was never sure that going to war against the United States was a good idea. When he was congratulated on the success of the attack, he said, "I fear we have only awakened a sleeping giant." He meant that Japan would now have to fight the huge power of the U.S., which it had not had to do before.

torpedo long, thin, underwater bomb that uses a propeller to push it along

CARRIER FORCES

Aircraft carriers are a wonder of the modern age. After Pearl Harbor, the United States' carrier forces helped win the war against Japan in the Pacific. Today, the United States has the greatest carrier force in the world. These carriers have been used very effectively in both Gulf wars. They launch jet aircraft on bombing missions into enemy territory. They have their own supply of **cruise missiles.** Russia, Great Britain, France, and other nations also have carrier forces. They use them to back up their military forces in trouble spots around the world.

Aircraft carriers can travel to almost anywhere on the planet to help out a nation's troops.

The U.S. aircraft carrier *John F. Kennedy* passes through the Caribbean.

SWORDFISH

Biplanes still operated during World War II. This British Fairey *Swordfish* was a carrier-based **torpedo** bomber. In 1941 a **squadron** of *Swordfish* helped to destroy the German battleship *Bismarck.* This was the biggest ship in the German navy at the time. Sinking the ship was very important to the British.

ammunition   guns and explosive items such as bombs

TOP SHIPS

A large, modern aircraft carrier is more than 1,000 feet (330 meters) long. It can carry about 90 aircraft. It takes over 3,000 people to look after the ship, and another 3,000 to look after the aircraft. Because aircraft carriers are so important, they usually travel with a fleet of other ships. Cruisers and destroyers (smaller, quicker, and well-armed ships) protect them from enemy ships, aircraft, and ground-launched missiles. Supply ships make sure they have fuel, **ammunition,** and food.

PHANTOM STRIKE

The McDonnell Douglas *F-4 Phantom* was one of the United States' most useful carrier-based fighter-bombers during the 1960s and 1970s. It carried several different missiles. Some missiles were meant for ground targets, while others were meant to protect it from enemy aircraft.

cruise missile   kind of guided missile that directs itself to its target

FLYING BOATS

Flying boats might look awkward, but because they can be landed on water, they have two great advantages over land-based planes. First, their pilots never have to worry about running out of runway for landing and takeoff. Second, flying boats can land facing any direction. It is difficult to land an ordinary plane on a runway if there are strong winds blowing across it. The first military flying boats were built during World War I. In the 1930s, aircraft designers made planes that were much bigger than those that could fly from land.

WATER WONDER

More American Catalina flying boats were made than any other kind of flying boat. The Catalina could operate from both land and sea, because it had **landing gears** as well as a boatlike hull and floats on its wings.

depth charge   bomb designed to explode under water and destroy a submarine

FLYING PORCUPINES

Great Britain, Japan, and the United States all had flying boat fleets during World War II. They were used for **reconnaissance,** rescue missions for pilots stranded in the sea, and for attacking enemy ships and **submarines.** The vast Short Sunderland flying boat shown here had a **crew** of thirteen. It dropped bombs, or **depth charges,** on enemy submarines. It was extremely good at fighting off enemy planes. German pilots called it the flying porcupine. It was a slow flyer (212 **mph**/341 km/h), but it could stay in the air for twenty hours. Unlike some flying boats, the Sunderland could only land and take off from water.

A Sunderland flying boat being repaired during World War II.

UNDERWATER PLANES

During World War II, Japan and the United States used submarines as **aircraft carriers.** The Japanese submarines carried three **torpedo** bombers. The submarine was designed to launch surprise attacks on the West Coast of the United States, but it was never used to do this.

EYES IN THE SKY

BALLOONS

Since warfare began, army commanders have wanted to be able to see what their enemy is doing. By the year 600, the Chinese had invented huge kites to lift a man into the air to see much farther than anyone on the ground. In 1783 a Frenchman named Jacques Charles invented the **hydrogen** balloon. French army commanders quickly started using the balloons. Hydrogen balloons were used to spy on enemy armies during the Napoleonic Wars in the late 1700s and early 1800s. These balloons could be blown anywhere by the wind, so they were tied down to keep them in one place. Balloons like these continued to be used throughout the 1800s and then in the early 1900s, during World War I.

hydrogen   element that is usually a gas with no color or smell

SPOTTER PLANES

The **reconnaissance** balloon was **obsolete** once powered flight was invented. Balloons were already **vulnerable** to powerful, long-range **artillery**. They were easy targets for fighter planes. One of the first reconnaissance planes was the British *BE 2*, used in World War I. It was a slow and steady flyer, which made it good for spotting enemy movements from the sky. This also made it very easy to shoot down. Some of the reconnaissance planes used in World War II were specially built for the job. The weird and wonderful World War II Blohm & Voss *Bv 141* had a special cabin that allowed the **crew** to see from all sides.

The strange shape of the Blohm & Voss *Bv 141* reconnaissance plane.

WOODEN PLANE

This British De Havilland *Mosquito* was one of the most successful reconnaissance aircraft of World War II. Because it was made of wood, it was very light. It could outrun any German fighter—until the arrival of the Messerschmidt *Me 262* jet in late 1944.

obsolete   old-fashioned, out-of-date

SEEING SOUND

The shock wave created as an aircraft breaks the sound barrier is sometimes seen for a split-second as a cloud of moisture. This amazing picture of an *F/A-18 Hornet* shows that moment, which is heard as a boom.

COLD WAR SPIES

In the **Cold War** between the Soviet Union and the United States and its **allies** after World War II, special aircraft were developed by both sides to spy on the enemy. One of the most famous was the United States' *U2*. It could not fly fast, and pilots hoped that flying at **altitudes** up to 80,000 feet (24,400 meters) would keep it safe from attack. This did not always work, and some *U2s* were shot down by missiles. Another American **reconnaissance** plane was the Lockheed *SR-71 Blackbird*. Some people think it is the most beautiful jet ever made. The *Blackbird* was loaded with **radar** and photography equipment. It was too fast for fighters and missiles to shoot down.

A Lockheed SR-71 Blackbird shoots through the sky.

TECH TALK

Pilots call the speed of sound Mach 1. Mach 2 is twice the speed of sound. This word is named after the Austrian physicist Ernst Mach. He carried out important work in aircraft science.

MOBILE RADAR

This jet carries a huge radar bowl on its back. Such aircraft are known as AWACS planes. This stands for Airborne Warning and Control System. During the Cold War, they kept a lookout for unexpected missile attacks.

SUBMARINE SPOTTERS

Both sides in the Cold War built special reconnaissance planes to hunt **submarines.** The British-built *Nimrod* was one of these aircraft. The *Nimrod* could fly twelve-hour missions without refueling. It had several detection devices to spot submarines, including one that was dragged through the sea under the aircraft. The *Nimrod* was equipped with antisubmarine mines, bombs, and **torpedoes.** Today, **satellites** and pilotless planes provide a lot of useful military information on other countries. The manned reconnaissance plane may soon be **obsolete.**

satellite object that circles Earth

ATTACK AND SUPPORT

Soldiers have had to put up with attack from the air since the days of World War I. Slow **biplane** fighters would fire **machine guns** from above. This was called strafing, which comes from a German word meaning "punish." But although it was effective, strafing enemy **trenches** was a highly dangerous job. Many planes were shot down, or their pilots were badly injured by ground fire.

STUKA SIREN

This German dive bomber from World War II had special sirens fitted to its wings. When it dived down to drop its single bomb, the sirens gave a high-pitched sound that was meant to spread panic among the soldiers below.

GROUND ATTACK

In World War II, ground attack aircraft included the German *Stuka* and Soviet *Shturmovik*. They caused panic among the troops and tank **crews** they were sent to attack.

cannon   weapon similar to a machine gun, but using larger bullets

The Soviet *Ilyushin Il-2 Shturmovik* was one of the most successful ground attack aircraft of World War II. The Soviets built a lot of them and armed them with heavy cannons. They attacked German tanks and other armored vehicles.

THUNDERBOLT

Today, ground attack aircraft are still an important part of warfare. The *A-10 Thunderbolt* is one of the most well known. It was used in both Gulf wars. It is a slow, clumsy-looking airplane, but it is built to hold up against enemy fire. The pilot is surrounded by heavy armor. It is highly **maneuverable** and can make very tight turns. The Thunderbolt carries more than 7.5 tons (6.8 metric tons) of weapons, including cluster bombs and antitank missiles. It is also armed with a **cannon** that can fire 4,200 rounds per minute. That is 70 heavy cannon shells a second.

The *A-10 Thunderbolt* may look bulky, but it can make sharp turns.

trench   deep ditch dug to protect soldiers

PARACHUTES

The parachute was invented in the late 18th century. Parachute troops called paratroops were first used in combat during World War II. Soldiers could be dropped behind enemy lines, but a soldier floating slowly down was very **vulnerable.** Because of this, paratroops were usually dropped as low as possible to cut down on their time in the air.

The German army used paratroops to win a quick victory in Crete in 1941. British and American paratroops were dropped during the **D-Day** landings of 1944. Today, soldiers on the ground carry surface-to-air missiles that can easily bring down slow-moving aircraft. This means a huge parachute drop is unlikely, because it is far too dangerous.

PARATROOPER TRANSPORTER

German forces used a transporter plane, the Junkers *Ju-52* (below), on the island of Crete to launch a surprise attack against the British during World War II. It was used in other early German victories in the war, too.

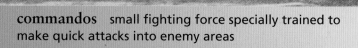

This Soviet *TB 3* was used to drop parachute troops.

commandos   small fighting force specially trained to make quick attacks into enemy areas

GLIDERS

Gliders, or airplanes without engines, were used by both sides in World War II. Towed by bombers, they carried supplies and troops. A large glider could even carry a tank. But gliders were very slow and crashed easily upon landing.

One of the most famous uses of gliders was in 1943. Germany's Italian **ally** Benito Mussolini was held captive by his own government. Germany's Adolf Hitler sent German **commandos** to rescue him. Gliders landed silently by the mountaintop hotel where Mussolini was being held. Then, troops stormed into the building. The attack was such a surprise that not a single shot was fired. Mussolini was flown away in a small German **reconnaissance** plane.

D-DAY GLIDER
This Airspeed *Horsa* glider was used to carry **Allied** troops during the June 1944 D-Day landings. A bad landing could mean all aboard were killed.

D-Day June 6, 1944—the day that the Allied invasion of mainland Europe began along the northern coast of France in World War II

45

HELICOPTERS

The ground attack aircraft has a serious rival—the helicopter. The first helicopters were invented in the mid-1930s. They cannot fly as fast as airplanes, but they can take off and land in small spaces. They can also hover, or stay in one place in the air, and are very **maneuverable.** During World War II, the U.S. Navy began to use helicopters for rescue missions at sea. Military helicopters are still used this way today. They also quickly carry wounded soldiers from the battlefield for medical attention.

MEDEVACS

About 7,000 of these Bell *Huey* helicopters flew in Vietnam for "dust offs" (dropping troops into enemy territory) and for "medevacs" (rescuing soldiers in need of medical aid).

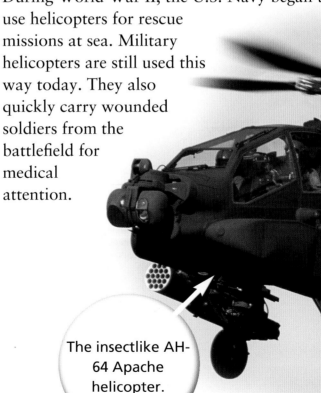

The insectlike AH-64 Apache helicopter.

EASY TARGETS

Helicopters were first used in great numbers in the Vietnam War (1955–1975). Bell *Hueys* and Boeing Vertol *Chinooks* were used to carry

supplies and to take troops into battle. These helicopters were able to take soldiers across land that ordinary vehicles could not get through. But helicopters had a downside, too. They were easy to shoot down—even by rifle or **machine-gun** fire.

Today, helicopters are also used as attack craft. The Boeing *AH-64 Apache* attack helicopter pictured here has **radar-controlled** missiles and guns for ground targets. It also has air-to-air missiles to protect it from other aircraft.

AIR CARRIER

Boeing Vertol *CH-47C Chinook* transport helicopters were used in Vietnam. They were important, too, in both Gulf wars. They carried troops and equipment to places that were hard to get to any other way.

The Lockheed *C-130 Hercules* was one of the first specially designed military transport aircraft. First used in 1956, more than 2,000 have now been built. There are more to come. The Hercules is also used as a **civilian** transporter. It can transport supplies such as food or medical aid to the world's trouble spots.

TRANSPORTERS

Some of the biggest aircraft ever built have been designed to carry troops and equipment across the world to distant battlefields. The first transporters were modified passenger planes, such as the German *Ju-52* or the American *DC-3 Dakota*. Both were used with great success during World War II. Even larger transporters were designed during the **Cold War**. Military forces still use these today.

BIG MOUTH

One of the largest transporters is the Lockheed *C-5 Galaxy*. This huge, jet-powered aircraft can carry 415 troops or 137 tons (124.3 metric tons) of equipment on its twin decks. It has 28 wheels to spread its huge weight over the ground. This makes it easier to land and take off from rough airstrips near a **front line.** Even fully loaded, it can fly about 3,500 miles (5,500 kilometers) in a single journey.

The American *C-5 Galaxy* transporter can carry a huge load.

Find out more about the Ju-52 on page 44.

FLYING TANKER

Some transporters are just huge fuel tankers, such as this Boeing *KC-135 Stratotanker.* It first flew in the 1950s and has been used by the U.S. Air Force ever since. It carries 61 tons (55.3 metric tons) of fuel.

Waiting fighters or bombers refuel in midair using a long pipe at the back of the aircraft. These tankers are very **vulnerable,** so they operate at 50,000 ft (15,000 m). This keeps them out of reach of most fighters and enemy missiles.

TECHNOLOGY

In less than 100 years, air weapons have changed almost completely. The first warplanes carried small handheld bombs that could do very little damage.

ADVANCES IN TECHNOLOGY

By 1945 one bomber could destroy a city with a single **atomic bomb.** Today, a single bomber packed with atomic weapons could destroy an entire country and millions of its citizens. The first bombs were steel cylinders packed with explosives. They blew up when they hit the ground. Nothing guided them down once they had been dropped, and they often missed their target.

BOUNCING BOMB

This famous bomb (shown being dropped below) from World War II was designed by British scientist Barnes Wallace. Its target was the huge concrete dams in Germany's industrial center. The bomb bounced like a ball across the water over nets placed in front of the dams.

A modern jet surrounded by its weapons **payload.**

payload   load carried by an aircraft. This load is the purpose of the flight.

GUIDED MISSILES

Today's military aircraft have guided missiles and "smart" bombs to attack targets on the ground. Weapons like this are directed to their targets by electronic **guidance** systems. These can be onboard TV cameras or heat and **radar** tracking devices.

The Hellfire is a American missile that can be dropped by an aircraft. Soldiers on the ground or helicopters circling nearby guide it to its target. The idea is to make the most of an expensive weapon and cut down on the number of **civilians** who are hit. But smart bombs do not always work. If they miss, many civilians can be killed.

MOAB

During the war in Afghanistan in 2002, U.S. forces dropped the biggest nonnuclear bombs available: the MOABs, or Massive Ordnance Air Bursts. These 11-ton (10-metric-ton) cylinders, such as the one below, carry a huge load that explodes above ground. They release a force big enough to knock over tanks and kill any soldiers within several thousand feet.

WATCH OUT ABOVE

Ever since aircraft were first used in combat, their targets on the ground have been trying to fire back at them. Ground-to-air guns are usually called **antiaircraft guns.** They were first used to shoot down enemy **reconnaissance** balloons. When the balloons went higher to escape the bullets, the men in them could not see what was happening on the ground. During World War I, antiaircraft guns were used against aircraft and zeppelins. They did not shoot many down, though. Hitting a fast-moving target high up in the sky was not easy.

A Sea Sparrow surface-to-air missile (SAM) launched from a carrier.

GETTING CLOSER

During World War II, German scientists developed a new kind of explosive weapon called the surface-to-air missile (SAM). It was a bomb that could move under its own power, rather than just dropping through the air. The first SAMs were either point-and-fire weapons with no **guidance** or were radio-controlled. By the 1950s, SAMs had been invented that followed the heat given out by an aircraft's engines. Today, antiaircraft SAMs pick up on **radar** signals from an enemy aircraft or have small TV cameras in their noses that allow people to guide them into their target. Some SAMs are so small they can be carried by a soldier.

MULTIBARREL MAYHEM

Bullets are still used to shoot at enemy aircraft. This Russian *ZSU 30-4* tracks its target via radar and shoots all four barrels at once in a continuous stream of deadly fire.

TECH TALK

Radar

Radar equipment sends a strong radio signal into the sky. If the signal hits a plane, it bounces back to the radar. This signal shows up its position on a TV screen.

A British Harrier pilot ejects just before the plane crashes.

BAIL OUT!

In the early days of air warfare, pilots did not carry parachutes. This was to stop pilots from bailing out rather than trying to land their expensive flying machines in one piece. Zeppelin **crews** did not carry parachutes, either. Although they were very big, zeppelins could only lift a small load. The people in charge thought it was more important to carry bombs than parachutes.

By World War II, there was much more concern about keeping pilots safe. Parachutes were given to pilots in almost all air forces. If a plane was badly damaged, a pilot could flip back the **cockpit** cover and jump to safety.

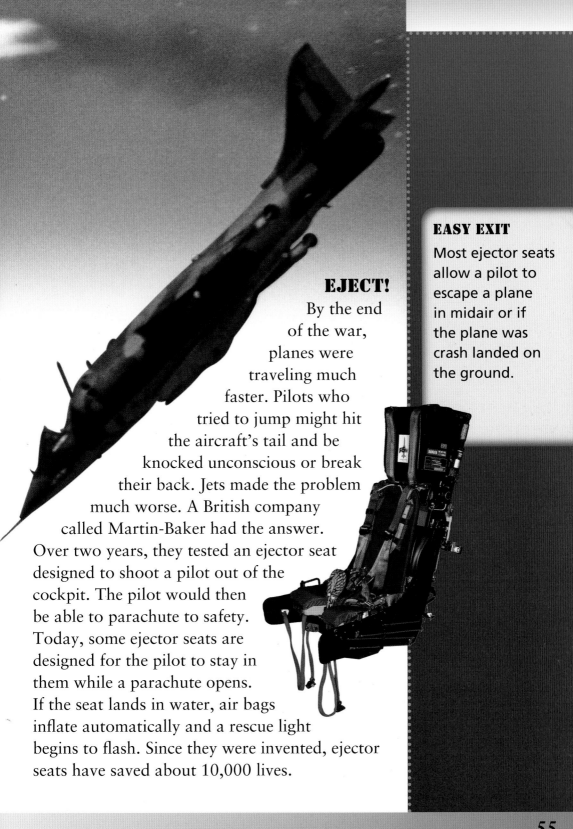

EJECT!

By the end of the war, planes were traveling much faster. Pilots who tried to jump might hit the aircraft's tail and be knocked unconscious or break their back. Jets made the problem much worse. A British company called Martin-Baker had the answer. Over two years, they tested an ejector seat designed to shoot a pilot out of the cockpit. The pilot would then be able to parachute to safety. Today, some ejector seats are designed for the pilot to stay in them while a parachute opens. If the seat lands in water, air bags inflate automatically and a rescue light begins to flash. Since they were invented, ejector seats have saved about 10,000 lives.

EASY EXIT

Most ejector seats allow a pilot to escape a plane in midair or if the plane was crash landed on the ground.

INTO THE FUTURE

RAPTOR

This Lockheed Martin *F-22A Raptor* is the latest type of American fighter jet. It has a **stealth** design to make it almost invisible on **radar**. It is extremely fast and maneuverable. All its weapons are stored inside its **fuselage**. This reduces the chance of it being spotted by enemy radar.

Predicting the future is always difficult. What fuel will military aircraft use, for example, when oil supplies run out? **Hydrogen** gas is one possibility. For now, it is too dangerous to use. In 10 or 50 years, scientists might have invented an engine that can safely use it.

IMPROVING TECHNOLOGY

As computers continue to improve, they will take over more and more flying and weapons-firing tasks from the pilot. Many plane designers are trying to improve existing fighters and bombers, rather than to introduce new aircraft. But some revolutionary new designs are being tested right now.

LATEST DEVELOPMENTS

Modern jets have become more difficult to **maneuver** because they fly so much faster than before. In World War I, a pilot could make a turn in less than half the time of a pilot in a jet plane today. Both the American Rockwell *MBB X-31* research plane and the Russian Sukhoi *S-37 Berkut* fighter overcame this problem by using an amazing new technique called **thrust** vectoring. Adjustable paddles of super-heat-resistant material are placed on the jet exhaust so that the thrust can be directed almost anywhere. This makes the jet very **agile.** It is able, for example, to turn very tight loops, almost seeming to somersault.

PILOTLESS PLANES

The pilotless *RQ-4A Global Hawk* (below) may be the future of combat flying. The pilot controlling a plane like this would be sitting elsewhere, far from danger.

Is this the future? The Russian Sukhoi *S-37 Berkut.*

Find out more about stealth bombers on pages 30 and 31.

AIRCRAFT FACTS

Warplanes have been with us for almost a century. They changed drastically between World War I, World War II, and today. The aircraft in the tables below are all typical of their time. The Sopwith *Camel* flew in World War I, the *P-51 Mustang* flew in World War II, and the Lockheed Martin *F-16* is used in combat today.

In 1944 Flight-Sergeant Nicholas Alkemade fell 5,485 meters (18,000 feet) without a parachute from a blazing bomber—and lived.

PERFORMANCE

	Sopwith Camel	P-51	F-16
Top speed	112 **mph** (180 km/h)	437 mph (703 km/h)	Mach 2 (twice the speed of sound)
Maximum **altitude**	19,000 ft (5,790 m)	41,900 ft (12,770 m)	50,000 ft (15,239 m)
Range	300 mi (483 km)	2,080 mi (3,350 km)	2,360 mi (3,800 km)

The Sopwith *Camel* was the best fighter plane of World War I, but it was tricky to fly. More pilots were killed while learning to fly it than were killed flying it in combat.

The youngest person ever to qualify as a military pilot was Thomas Dobney, who was fifteen years and five months old in 1941. He was fourteen when he joined the British air force, but he lied about his age and got away with it.

58   **UP TO SPEED**   horsepower   technical term for a unit of measurement used to show the power of an engine

TECHNOLOGY

	Sopwith Camel	P-51	F-16
Wings	Biplane	Monoplane	Swept-back wings
Engine	130 **horsepower** **internal combustion** engine turns a **propeller**	1,695 horsepower internal combustion engine turns a propeller	Jet engine produces **thrust**
Crew	One, in open **cockpit**	One, in enclosed **Plexiglas** cockpit	One or two, in enclosed Plexiglas cockpit with ejector seat(s)
Shape	Chunky shape. Fixed **landing gear** that could not be raised inside the plane.	Smoother shape. Retractable landing gear raised into plane after takeoff.	Ultra-smooth design, including retractable landing gear to cut down wind resistance

WEAPONS

	Sopwith Camel	P-51	F-16
Guns	Two **machine guns** mounted behind the propeller	Six heavy machine guns mounted inside the wings	Single **cannon** in the nose
Bombs	None	Two large bombs or five small rockets	Up to nine air-to-air or air-to-surface missiles or bombs guided by **radar,** laser, or infrared **guidance** systems

Find out more about these aircraft on pages 12, 14, and 17.

internal combustion   when fuel burns inside an engine

FIND OUT MORE

ORGANIZATIONS

Air Museum—Planes of Fame Headquarters
7000 Merrill Ave. # 17
Chino, CA 91710
(909) 597-3722

National Warplane Museum
Elmira-Corning Regional Airport
17 Aviation Drive
Horseheads, NY 14845
director@wingsofeagles.com

Smithsonian National Air and Space Museum
6th St. & Independence Ave. SW
Washington, D.C. 20560
info@si.edu

BOOKS

Chant, Christopher. *Military Aircraft*. Langhorne, Pa.: Chelsea House, 1999.

Doyle, Kevin. *Aircraft Carriers*. Minneapolis, Minn.: Lerner Publishing Group, 2003.

Hansen, Ole Steen. *Modern Military Aircraft*. New York: Crabtree Publishing, 2003.

WORLD WIDE WEB

If you want to find out more about military aircraft, you can search the Internet using keywords like these:

aircraft + bombers
"Douglas Bader"
"ejector seats"
"Spitfire"

Make your own keywords using headings or words from this book. The search tips on the next page will help you to find the most useful websites.

SEARCH TIPS

There are billions of pages on the Internet, so it can be difficult to find exactly what you want to find. If you just type in "aircraft" on a search engine such as Google, you will get a list of millions of web pages. These search skills will help you find useful websites more quickly.

- Use simple keywords, not whole sentences.
- Use two to six keywords in a search.
- Be precise—only use names of people, places, or things.
- If you want to find words that go together, put quote marks around them—for example, "world speed record."
- Use the advanced section of your search engine.
- Use the "+" sign between keywords to find pages with all these words.

WHERE TO SEARCH

SEARCH ENGINE

A search engine looks through millions of web pages and lists all sites that match the search words. The best matches are at the top of the list, on the first page. Try **google.com**.

SEARCH DIRECTORY

A search directory is like a library of websites. You can try searching by keyword or subject and then browse through the different sites as you would look through books on a library shelf. A good example is **yahooligans.com**.

GLOSSARY

agile   able to move quickly and gracefully

aircraft carrier   warship that carries fighter planes to near their target

allies/Allies   countries that support one another in a war. The name Allies was used for Great Britain, France, the United States, and other countries fighting on the same side (against Germany) in World War I and World War II.

altitude   height above sea level

ammunition   bullets and explosive items such as bombs

antiaircraft guns   guns made to defend against an air attack

artillery   large, land-based guns

atomic bomb   bomb with violent explosive power made by scientists

biplane   plane with two sets of wings, one above the other

cannon   weapon similar to a machine gun, but using larger bullets

civilian   person not in the military

cockpit   area where the crew sits and controls the airplane

Cold War   years between 1946 and 1989 when the Soviet Union and the United States and its allies did not like or trust each other

commandos   small fighting force specially trained to make quick attacks into enemy areas

crankshaft   part of an engine that transfers the power generated in the piston to the propeller

crew   people who operate the aircraft

cruise missile   kind of guided missile that directs itself to its target

D-Day   June 6, 1944—day that the Allied invasion of mainland Europe began along the northern coast of France in World War II

depth charge   bomb designed to explode under water and destroy a submarine

front line   place on a battlefield where the two sides meet

fuselage   main body of an aircraft

guidance   way of making sure a weapon hits its target

high-performance   jet that can fly faster and higher and with greater maneuverability than most other jets

horsepower   technical term for a unit of measurement used to show the power of an engine

hydrogen   element that is usually a gas with no color or smell. It can be used for different scientific purposes, such as balloons and bombs.

ignite   start to burn

incendiary bomb   bomb that bursts into flames, rather than exploding

incendiary bullet   bullet that bursts into flames when fired from a gun

interceptor   type of jet fighter that can climb and fly very quickly to cut off enemy aircraft

intercontinental ballistic missile (ICBM)   missile that flies into space or very high up so that it can travel across continents

internal combustion when fuel burns inside an engine

landing gears wheels and lower part of an aircraft that support it when it takes off or lands

lift force that lifts a plane into the air

machine gun gun that can fire bullets very quickly in a row

maneuverable able to turn or change direction easily

monoplane plane with one wing on each side

mph (miles per hour) number of miles traveled in one hour

nozzle pipe that directs the thrust of a jet engine

obsolete old-fashioned, out-of-date

payload load carried by an aircraft. This load is the purpose of the flight.

piston piece of metal that fits tightly in a tube in which it is moved up and down by a small explosion to give movement to other parts of the engine

Plexiglas transparent, tough, plasticlike resin used instead of glass to make windows or cockpit covers in aircraft

propeller spinning blade that pulls an aircraft through the air

radar way of finding out the position of objects, such as aircraft, by using radio signals

reconnaissance keeping watch on an enemy's movements and strength

rocket-propelled has an engine that works by burning fuel and oxygen together in a combustion chamber to produce thrust

satellite object that circles Earth

silo storage site

simulator device that copies the conditions of an actual situation

speed of sound how fast sound travels

squadron fighting group or unit in an air force

stealth designed to not be seen

strategic bomber bomber that attacks an enemy's home, rather than being used on the battlefield

submarine ship that can stay under water

swept-back wings wings that make a V or triangular shape against the body of an airplane

swing-wing wing that pivots backward or forward from the main body of the aircraft, depending on how it is being flown

test pilot pilot who flies experimental or untested aircraft

thrust force produced by a jet aircraft to propel it through the sky

torpedo long, thin, underwater bomb that uses a propeller to push it along

trench deep ditch dug to protect soldiers

triplane plane with three sets of wings on each side

turret low dome containing machine guns projecting from an aircraft. It can usually swivel so that the guns can be fired in any direction.

vertical straight upward

vulnerable easy to attack or shoot down, not well-protected

INDEX